WHOOO! GIGGLES AND SHIVERS

More Lightly Spooky, Funny Friendly Tales for Brave Young Readers (Ages 5-8)

VOL-2

Rachel Wintergreen

ISBN: 9789355252814

Author: Rachel Wintergreen

Contact: storyline@svakrta.com

Website: www.svakrta.com

svakrta STORYLINE

Introduction

Whooo! Welcome back, brave adventurers!

Did you survive the friendly frights from our first book? Are you ready for even MORE giggles and shivers?

You asked for it, and here it is—Volume 2 of Whooo! series of our spooky-but-not-too-spooky adventures! Inside these pages, you'll find 10 brand-new tales bursting with lovable monsters, mysterious bells, magical creatures, and enchanted surprises that will make you smile and shiver at the same time.

This time around, you'll meet monsters who are more scared than scary, ghost animals on important missions, and solve puzzles that will tickle your brain and your funny bone!

Remember—these creatures might look a little strange, and the mysteries might seem a bit spooky, but there's always a happy ending waiting. After all, the best adventures are the ones where you make unexpected friends and discover that not everything that goes "bump" in the night is something to fear!

So fluff up those pillows, grab your flashlight (you might need it for clues!), and prepare yourself for another round of magical mischief and heartwarming hauntings!

Ready for round two?

Let's jump back in... if you're brave enough!

TABLE OF CONTENTS

LITTLE MUMMY GHOST AND THE MISSING PUMPKIN

Halloween night sparkled in Willow Hollow! Orange and purple lights twinkled from every porch, and the sweet smell of candy corn filled the air.

Brother and Sister Max and Lily had just finished carving the most amazing jack-o'-lantern on their entire street. It had big, triangle eyes and a zigzag smile that looked friendly and fun.

"Wow!" Max said, stepping back to admire their work. "This is our best pumpkin ever!"

Lily clapped her hands. "All the trick-or-treaters are going to love it! Let's put it on the porch."

Max carefully picked up their beautiful jack-o'-lantern and carried it toward the front door. But just as they reached the porch...

WHOOOOSH!

A cloud of dusty wind swirled around them like a mini tornado!

When the dust settled, their precious pumpkin was completely gone!

"Oh no!" Lily gasped. "Where did it go?"

Max looked around frantically. "It was right here in my hands!"

They searched their porch, their yard, and behind the bushes. All they found were a few pumpkin seeds scattered on the ground and strange, wobbly footprints leading away from their house.

"This is a real Halloween mystery," Max said, studying the odd tracks.

Lily grabbed her flashlight. "Then let's solve it! Those footprints will lead us right to our pumpkin!"

Max and Lily followed the wobbly footprints past houses decorated with friendly ghosts, silly skeletons, and smiling bats. The trail twisted down sidewalks and around corners until it ended at the quiet little park at the end of their street.

The air smelled dusty and old, like an attic that hadn't been opened in years. Sparkly dust floated in Lily's flashlight beam.

"Whoever took our pumpkin must be hiding nearby," Max whispered.

Suddenly, they heard a sound from behind some hay bales.

Giggle-giggle-sniff.

It was a small, sad laugh.

Max and Lily tiptoed closer and peeked around the hay. There, floating in the moonlight, was the tiniest mummy they had ever seen!

Old, dusty bandages wrapped around his small, ghostly body, but they kept coming loose and dragging on the ground. And the strangest part? He was wearing their jack-o'-lantern on his head like a helmet!

The little mummy giggled again, making the pumpkin's carved smile bounce up and down.

"Hey!" Lily called out. "That's our jack-o'-lantern!"

The little mummy froze. Then, in the tiniest, most embarrassed voice, he squeaked, "Oops."

Max stepped forward with a friendly smile. "Hi there. I'm Max, and this is my sister Lily. What's your name?"

The mummy ghost lifted the pumpkin just enough for them to see his glowing eyes underneath. "I'm Zuzu," he said shyly. "And I'm really sorry. I didn't mean to steal your pumpkin."

"Then why did you take it?" Lily asked gently.

Zuzu floated down to sit on a hay bale. More of his old bandages unwound and fell to the ground like sad ribbons.

"Look at me," he sighed. "My mummy wrappings are so old and worn out, they won't stay wrapped! I don't look scary, I just look messy."

Max tilted his head. "So you took our pumpkin because...?"

"Because when I wear it, I have a perfect spooky face!" Zuzu turned his head, making the jack-o'-lantern spin. "See? Now I look like a real Halloween monster!"

Max and Lily couldn't help but smile. With the big pumpkin sitting on his little head, Zuzu looked more adorable than scary.

"Oh, Zuzu," Lily said kindly. "You don't look scary at all. You look cute!"

Zuzu's shoulders slumped. "That's exactly the problem! I just wanted a real Halloween like everyone else. I wanted to be fun and spooky."

Lily looked at Max, and Max looked at Lily. They both had the same idea at the same time.

"What if we helped you have the best Halloween ever?" Max asked with a big grin.

Zuzu's eyes lit up like tiny stars. "You... you would help me? Even though I took your pumpkin?"

"Of course!" Lily said. "That's what friends do! But first, we need our jack-o'-lantern back so we can put it on our porch for the trick-or-treaters."

Zuzu carefully floated the pumpkin off his head and handed it to Max. "Here. I'm really, really sorry I took it without asking."

"It's okay," Max said. "Everyone makes mistakes. Now let's get you ready for Halloween!"

Back at Max and Lily's house, they gathered supplies: fresh white fabric strips, soft tape, and some sparkly glue for decoration.

"Hold still, Zuzu," Lily said as she and Max carefully began wrapping bright, clean bandages around their new friend.

"Ooh, these feel so much better!" Zuzu wiggled happily. "They're soft and cozy!"

Max added a tiny orange bow made from Halloween ribbon on top of Zuzu's head as a finishing touch.

"There!" Lily announced. "Now you look like the perfect little mummy ghost!"

Zuzu floated over to look in the hallway mirror and gasped with joy. "I look amazing! And look, my bandages stay on!"

He spun happily in the air, and not a single bandage came loose.

"Now I'm ready for Halloween!" Zuzu cheered.

Max grinned. "You sure are! Want to go trick-or-treating with us?"

That night, Max, Lily, and Zuzu went trick-or-treating all around the neighborhood.

Zuzu floated happily beside them, his brand-new white bandages glowing brightly under all the Halloween lights.

And Zuzu discovered something even better than trying to scare people, he could make them smile! When he waved his bandaged arms or did little flips in the air, kids would giggle and clap.

"I love your mummy costume!" a little girl in a princess outfit exclaimed.

"Thank you!" Zuzu beamed. "My friends helped me make it!"

A boy dressed as a superhero gave Zuzu's bandaged hand a high-five. "You're the friendliest mummy I've ever met!"

When the night grew late, they returned home. Max and Lily's glowing jack-o'-lantern sat on the front porch, greeting the last trick-or-treaters with its bright smile. Zuzu floated next to it, helping hand out candy to the younger kids.

"This was the best Halloween ever!" Zuzu said as they watched the last group of trick-or-treaters head home.

"Why do you think that is?" Lily asked with a knowing smile.

Zuzu thought for a moment, then his eyes glowed with understanding. "Because being kind and making friends is way better than just trying to be scary!"

Max nodded. "And because the best part of Halloween isn't scaring people.

It's sharing the fun with friends!"

"Plus," Lily added, "We got an awesome new friend!"

The three friends laughed together under the full moon, and their jack-o'-lantern glowed warm and welcoming, as if saying, "Everyone is welcome here."

From that Halloween on, Zuzu visited Max and Lily

all the time. Every year, they worked together to create even more special jack-o'-lanterns to welcome visitors and spread Halloween cheer throughout Willow Hollow.

The best costumes aren't the scariest ones, they're the ones that help us make new friends.

THE GHOST THAT SNEEZES

Lucy and Max loved visiting Grandpa Joe's old Victorian house. It had creaky floors, hidden doors, and mysterious trunks full of forgotten treasures. But their favorite place was the dusty attic, where adventure hid in every corner.

One cool October afternoon, golden leaves danced outside the attic window as Lucy and Max climbed the creaky stairs. Sunlight streamed through the wooden boards, making the floating dust look like tiny fairies.

"I wonder what we'll find today!" Max said, pushing aside a big wooden chest.

Lucy spotted something interesting against the far wall. A tall, old mirror covered in dust and cobwebs. "Look at this! I can barely see my reflection."

She rolled up her sleeve and started wiping the glass clean.

That's when it happened.

"AHHH-CHOOO!"

The loudest sneeze ever echoed through the attic! It was so powerful that Lucy's hair flew back, books tumbled off shelves, and dust clouds exploded everywhere.

Lucy and Max jumped back with wide eyes.

The mirror started shimmering like water, and suddenly a face appeared in the glass! A young, wispy ghost with kind eyes and a worried expression!

The ghost waved apologetically from inside the mirror. "Oh no! I'm so sorry! I didn't mean to scare you!"

Lucy's eyes went wide. "Did... did you just sneeze?"

The ghost nodded sadly. "My name is Finn. I've been stuck in this mirror for weeks and–"

"ACHOO!"

Another enormous sneeze shook the attic, sending more dust flying.

Max rubbed his nose. "Whoa! That's some sneeze!"

Finn's ghostly form flickered miserably. "Tell me about it! Every time I sneeze, I can't escape the mirror. I think all this dust is making me sick!"

Lucy felt sorry for the friendly ghost. "That sounds terrible! Why can't you just float away?"

Finn sighed. "Every time I sneeze, it's like a magnet pulls me back to the mirror. Halloween is tomorrow! I should be outside having fun saying 'Boo!' but instead I'm stuck here saying 'Achoo!'"

Max and Lucy looked at each other, then back at poor Finn.

"Don't worry," Lucy said firmly. "We'll help you stop sneezing!"

Over the next hour, they tried lots of clever solutions.

First, Max grabbed Grandpa's old fan to blow the dust away. But when he turned it on, Finn sneezed so hard the fan flew across the room and knocked over a stack of books!

"Sorry!" Finn called out from the mirror, looking embarrassed.

Next, Lucy dug through her backpack and tried wrapping an old scarf around Finn's nose. "Maybe this will filter out the dust."

But when Finn sneezed again, the scarf flew through the air like a ribbon and landed in a crumpled heap.

Max scratched his head. "This is trickier than I thought."

Then Lucy had an idea. "Wait! When Grandpa Joe has a scratchy throat, he always drinks tea with honey. He says Honey makes everything better!"

Finn looked uncertain. "But I'm a ghost. I don't think I can drink tea."

"Have you ever tried?" Max asked with a grin.

Finn thought about it. "Well... no. I guess I just assumed I couldn't."

The three friends tiptoed downstairs to the kitchen, where Grandpa Joe was napping in his favorite armchair.

Lucy carefully scooped out a spoonful of golden honey

from the jar. "Just try a tiny taste," she whispered to Finn, who was now following them in the reflection of the kitchen window.

Finn looked nervous and curious at the same time. He stuck out his ghostly tongue and barely touched the honey.

His eyes went wide with surprise. "Oh! It's warm and tingly and sweet!"

Finn took another small taste, then another.

Something amazing started happening. Finn's ghostly form glowed brighter and steadier. His nose stopped twitching constantly.

Lucy held her breath. "How do you feel?"

Finn concentrated for a moment, then broke into the biggest smile. "I... I think the tickle is gone! My nose doesn't feel stuffy anymore!"

Just then, Grandpa Joe stirred in his chair.

He yawned and stretched. "What are you kids up to?"

Finn quickly disappeared with a soft whoosh, but not before giving Lucy and Max a grateful thumbs-up in the window reflection.

"Just getting ready for Halloween, Grandpa!" Lucy said, trying not to giggle.

The next night, Lucy and Max were trick-or-treating around their neighborhood when they heard a familiar voice.

"Booooo! Happy Halloween!"

It was Finn! He floated happily through the streets, giving trick-or-treaters gentle, friendly scares that made them squeal with delight.

"We did it!" Lucy and Max whispered to each other as they watched Finn hide behind a fence to surprise a group of kids dressed as pirates.

"He looks so happy," Lucy agreed, waving at their ghost friend.

Finn spotted them and floated over with a huge grin. "Thank you both so much! This is the best Halloween ever! Now I can finally do what ghosts do best–have fun!"

"Just don't forget to visit us," Lucy told him. "The attic gets lonely without you."

Finn's eyes sparkled. "Are you kidding? I'll be back tomorrow! Though I'll bring my own honey next time."

From that day on, Lucy and Max had the coolest friend ever at Grandpa Joe's attic. Finn would appear in the old mirror, always ready for a new adventure or to help them explore the house's hidden secrets.

He told them stories about the neighborhood's friendly ghosts. He taught them how to make the old floorboards creak in musical patterns. He even helped them find Grandpa Joe's secret stash of peppermint candies hidden behind a loose board!

Finn never had another sneezing fit because Lucy and Max always remembered to bring him honey.

Sometimes the best friendships start with someone who needs a little help. And the greatest adventures happen when you're brave enough to reach out, even to a sneezing ghost stuck in an old mirror.

PUZZLE OF THE MIDNIGHT BELL

Every night at midnight, the antique bell in Willowbrook's town square rang out across the peaceful streets.

DONG, DONG, DONG!

The strange thing was, nobody was pulling the rope.

Emma and Jake lived across the street from the bell tower. They were both awake when the bell chimed at midnight. Whenever they peeked out their bedroom window, they saw the same thing: an empty tower, a still rope, and a bell that rang all by itself.

"It has to be a ghost," Emma said as they walked past the tower on their way to school one morning.

"Or maybe it's just broken," Jake replied, but he didn't sound sure.

Emma shook her head. "Jake, broken bells don't ring perfectly at midnight every single night for three months. That's not an accident."

That night, Emma had an idea. She tossed a small

pebble at Jake's window.

"Psst! Jake!" she whispered as he opened it. "Want to solve the mystery of the midnight bell?"

Jake rubbed his sleepy eyes. "Right now? It's almost midnight."

"Exactly! Grab your flashlight. We're going on a mystery-solving adventure!"

The two friends snuck out of their houses and tiptoed across the town square. The old bell tower stood tall and dark in the moonlight.

"I'm kind of scared," Jake said, staying close to Emma.

"Me too," she admitted. "But that's what makes it an adventure!"

They hid behind the fountain. The town square was so quiet they could hear their own heartbeats.

When the clock struck twelve, something amazing happened.

The air around the bell tower began to shimmer like summer heat waves. A soft, silvery glow appeared near the bell rope.

DONG, DONG, DONG!

The bell rang, but nobody was there!

"Did you see that shimmer?" Emma gasped.

Jake nodded, his eyes wide. "Something's up there!"

The next night, they returned with a plan. This time, Emma brought her mom's binoculars.

As midnight approached, they watched the tower

carefully. The strange glow appeared again, and the bell began to ring.

But through the binoculars, Emma saw something incredible.

"Jake!" she whispered excitedly. "It's not just a shimmer. It's a tiny ghost squirrel!"

"A what?" Jake grabbed the binoculars. Sure enough, there was the tiniest ghost squirrel he'd ever seen. It had a fluffy white tail and golden eyes that sparkled like stars. The little squirrel was using all its strength to pull on the bell rope.

When the bell stopped ringing, the ghost squirrel sat on the rope and sighed sadly.

Emma felt sorry for him right away. "Hello, little squirrel!" she called softly.

The ghost squirrel nearly fell off the rope in surprise. "You can see me?" he squeaked.

"We sure can!" Jake said. "I'm Jake, and this is Emma. What's your name?"

The squirrel puffed out his tiny chest proudly. "I'm Acorn, Keeper of the Great Golden Nut!"

Emma and Jake looked at each other. "The Great Golden Nut?" Emma asked.

Acorn's ears drooped sadly. "It was a magical acorn that glowed like sunshine. I buried it somewhere safe so long ago, but now I can't remember where!"

"Is that why you ring the bell every night?" Jake asked

gently.

Acorn nodded. “I hoped someone kind would hear it and help me search. But I’m a ghost now, so I can’t dig anymore. My paws just pass right through the dirt!”

Emma’s heart melted. “Oh, Acorn! We’ll help you find your special acorn!”

Acorn’s eyes filled with hope. “Really? You’d do that for me?”

“Of course!” Jake said. “That’s what friends do!”

Acorn tried hard to remember where he’d hidden his treasure. “It was near something that sparkled... something that made music when the wind blew...”

Emma took a deep breath and looked around the town square. “Something that sparkles and makes music... like water?”

“The fountain!” Jake shouted, pointing at the old stone fountain behind them.

Acorn’s eyes grew huge with joy. “Yes! YES! The fountain! I buried it near the fountain so I could hear the water!”

Emma and Jake immediately started searching around the fountain’s base. They looked behind bushes, under benches, and all around the stones.

“Here!” Emma called out. “The dirt looks different here, like it was dug up a long time ago!”

They carefully dug with their hands while Acorn floated nearby, bouncing with excitement.

"I found something!" Jake said, pulling something small from the ground.

It was the most beautiful acorn they'd ever seen. It glowed with a warm, golden light that made the whole town square feel magical.

"My Great Golden Nut!" Acorn cried tears of joy that sparkled like little stars. "Thank you! Thank you both so much!"

When Emma placed the glowing acorn in Acorn's tiny paws, something wonderful happened. The ghost squirrel's glow became brighter and brighter until he looked like a tiny, happy star.

"Now that I have my treasure back, I can finally rest," Acorn said with a big smile. "No more midnight bells! No more searching! Just sweet dreams and happy memories."

"Will we see you again?" Emma asked.

Acorn grinned. "Maybe in your dreams! And on nights when the moon is extra bright, you might see a little golden sparkle in the trees. I'll be watching over all the good things in town, especially my two best friends."

With that, Acorn's light grew softer and softer until he faded away with a contented sigh, leaving only the faint scent of autumn leaves and the warm feeling of having helped a friend.

Emma and Jake walked home together, tired but happy.

"That was the best mystery ever," Jake said.

"And the best part," Emma added, "is that now everyone in town can sleep peacefully at midnight."

From that night on, the bell tower stayed quiet at midnight. But on extra bright nights, Emma and Jake could see a tiny golden sparkle dancing in the oak trees around town, reminding them of their special friend and the night they solved the puzzle of the midnight bell.

THE MYSTERY OF THE PUMPKIN PATCH

Mia loved Halloween more than any other holiday. She adored the crisp fall air and the sound of golden leaves crunching underfoot. Every year, Farmer Joe held a contest for the biggest pumpkin in town, and this year, Mia knew she had found the winner.

It was huge, round, and the perfect shade of orange. "This is it!" Mia told her best friend Sam the day before the contest. "This pumpkin is definitely going to win!"

But when Mia arrived at the pumpkin patch early on Halloween morning, her heart nearly stopped.

The giant pumpkin was gone.

In its place was a glowing trail of footprints leading straight to the old, abandoned barn at the edge of the field.

Everyone said the barn was haunted, but Mia was determined. She was going to find her pumpkin, and not even a ghost story could stop her.

She took a deep breath and followed the glowing tracks, walking carefully until she reached the barn door. It creaked loudly as she pushed it open.

Inside, the air smelled like hay and something sweet, like pumpkin pie.

Then she saw it.

Her missing pumpkin was sitting in the middle of the barn, but it wasn't just sitting there. It had arms and legs sticking out of it!

Mia gasped loudly. "You're not a pumpkin. You're a ghost!"

The pumpkin-headed ghost was bouncing and spinning around. His big, round head wobbled dangerously before he caught it with both hands.

"Please don't be scared!" he squeaked in a wobbly, nervous voice.

Mia stepped forward cautiously. "Why did you take my pumpkin?"

The ghost shuffled his feet sheepishly. "I'm Oliver, and I'm really sorry. I lost my head."

Mia blinked. "You... lost your head?"

Oliver nodded, making the pumpkin wobble. "My ghost friends and I were playing hide-and-seek in October. I found the best hiding spot ever, but when I jumped out to yell 'Boo!' my ghost head just fell right off! I've been searching for a new one ever since."

Mia tilted her head. "Why didn't you just go find your

old head?"

Oliver sighed sadly. "I tried, but it rolled away somewhere, and I've been too embarrassed to ask anyone for help." He slumped down. "I just wanted to feel like a real ghost again."

Mia felt a pang of sympathy, but she also felt frustrated. "That's my winning pumpkin, though! I need it for the contest!"

Oliver sighed again. "I know, but without a head, I'm just a floating sheet."

Mia thought for a moment. Then she had an idea. "Wait! What if we find something else you can use as a head?"

Oliver perked up. "Really? You'd help me?"

"Of course!" Mia grinned. "But we need to hurry. The contest starts soon!"

Together, they searched the barn from top to bottom. They tried a wooden bucket, a hay bale, and even an old football helmet, but nothing worked quite right.

Then Mia spotted something in the corner. It was a beautiful paper lantern, bright and round with a warm, friendly glow. It was just the right size!

She picked it up and held it out to Oliver. "What about this?"

Oliver's eyes lit up. "It's perfect!"

Mia carefully placed the lantern where Oliver's head should be. The soft glow made him look warm and wonderfully ghostly.

Oliver spun around excitedly. “This feels amazing! I feel like myself again! Thank you, Mia!”

Mia beamed. “Now let’s get that pumpkin back to the contest!”

They rolled the giant pumpkin back to the patch just in time. When people saw it, they gasped in amazement. It was the biggest pumpkin anyone had ever seen!

Farmer Joe announced with a huge smile, “Looks like we have our winner!”

When Mia and Sam turned to thank Oliver, he was already floating away into the evening sky.

“Happy Halloween, Mia!” Oliver called out, his lantern head glowing softly in the moonlight.

Mia waved back happily. “Happy Halloween, Oliver!”

As Mia watched the town celebrate with pumpkin pie and candy, she smiled. She knew this Halloween would be one she’d remember forever. Not just because she won the contest, but because she made a new friend who needed help.

GHOSTLY GIGGLES OF PUMPKIN HOLLOW

Lily and Max loved Halloween more than any other day of the year. Every year, they dressed up in their scariest costumes and went trick-or-treating in their small town of Willow Creek. But this year was different. Their parents had one important rule: stay away from the old pumpkin field on the edge of town.

"Strange things happen there on Halloween night," their dad warned them. "People say the pumpkins move around on their own, and you can hear laughter in the wind."

Of course, Lily and Max thought that sounded amazing! So as soon as they collected enough candy from their neighbors, they headed straight to Pumpkin Hollow.

The night was chilly, and the full moon made everything glow silver. As they walked past the old, rusty gate, a gentle breeze carried the sound of distant giggles.

Lily grabbed Max's hand. "Did you hear that?"

Before Max could answer, something rolled toward them from the shadows. A small pumpkin was bouncing their way! Its carved mouth twisted into a silly grin, and it wobbled as it moved.

"Hello!" the pumpkin squeaked.

Lily and Max gasped!

"Oops! Sorry!" The pumpkin giggled. "I didn't mean to startle you. I'm Pip. Welcome to Pumpkin Hollow!"

Lily's eyes grew wide. "Did that pumpkin just talk?"

Max, feeling braver, crouched down. "How are you moving?"

Pip rolled on his little stem. "Oh, all the pumpkins in Pumpkin Hollow come to life on Halloween night! It's the best night of the year! Want to play with us?"

Lily and Max looked at each other with matching grins. This was the most magical Halloween ever!

Before they could answer, giggles filled the air all around them. Pumpkins of every size and shape bounced out from behind hay bales and fence posts, rolling and hopping like happy orange balls.

"Let's play pumpkin hide-and-seek!" called out a pumpkin slightly bigger than Pip.

"How do we play?" Max asked excitedly.

The pumpkins spun around with joy. "We hide, and you find us! Ready?"

Lily and Max loved hide-and-seek. They closed their eyes and counted to ten while the pumpkins giggled and rolled away into the darkness.

"Ready or not, here we come!" Lily shouted.

They searched behind tall hay bales, under a creaky old scarecrow, and inside hollow tree trunks. Every time they found a pumpkin, it would laugh and spin in circles before joining them to find the others.

Finally, only one pumpkin was left: Pip!

"Where could he be?" Max wondered, scratching his head.

Lily tapped her chin thoughtfully. "Hmm... if I were a tiny pumpkin, where would I hide?"

Then she noticed something odd. One of the biggest pumpkins in the patch was wiggling slightly.

She tiptoed over and knocked gently on its side.

"Boo!" Pip jumped out from behind the giant pumpkin. "You found me!"

All the other pumpkins cheered and rolled around in a happy circle. "Time for the Midnight Pumpkin Dance!"

"The what?" Max asked curiously.

Pip twirled. "When the moon is brightest on Halloween, we dance to celebrate! Join us!"

Before Lily and Max could even think about it, the pumpkins grabbed onto their stems like hands and started twirling, bouncing, and spinning in a magical dance.

The whole pumpkin patch glowed with enchanted light as they danced under the moon. Laughter filled the air, and for a wonderful moment, nothing else in the world mattered except joy and friendship.

Then suddenly, DONG! The old town clock struck midnight.

The pumpkins gasped. “Oh no! There’s not much time left!”

“Time for what?” Max asked.

Pip gave a sad little smile. “Time to go back to sleep until next Halloween!”

One by one, the pumpkins yawned and settled back onto the ground, their magic fading away. Soon, the whole field was silent, just an ordinary pumpkin patch once more.

Lily and Max blinked in surprise, standing in the middle of the quiet field. Had it all been a dream?

Then Max felt something in his pocket. He pulled out a small, glowing pumpkin seed.

Lily reached into her pocket and found one too.

“See you next Halloween,” came Pip’s voice, soft as a whisper on the wind.

The siblings walked home together, their bags full of candy and their hearts full of magic.

From that night on, every Halloween, Lily and Max would return to Pumpkin Hollow, hoping the pumpkins would wake up again.

And they always did. Because the children knew a wonderful secret: the pumpkins in Pumpkin Hollow weren't just ordinary pumpkins. They were magical, and they were waiting for friends to come play.

GHOST WHO BORROWED THE MOONLIGHT

Every night, the moon made everything in Willow Hollow sparkle with silver light. It helped kids catch fireflies after bedtime, made the rooftops shine, and turned the river into flowing diamonds.

But one night, something very strange happened.

The moon disappeared.

Not behind a cloud or hidden by shadows. It was just... gone.

Little Ben woke up in complete darkness. No soft glow through his window. No silvery light dancing on his walls.

"Whiskers?" he called, reaching for his orange cat.

Instead of purring, Whiskers jumped onto the windowsill and hissed at something outside.

Ben sat up quickly. "What's wrong, boy?"

Then he saw it.

Far away, near the old mansion at the edge of town,

something was glowing. It looked like moonlight, but it wasn't in the sky. The light was trapped inside a huge, bright jar on the mansion's roof!

Ben gasped. "Someone stole the moonlight!"

Whiskers meowed urgently and flicked his tail toward the door.

"You're right. We have to get it back!" Ben grabbed his flashlight and followed Whiskers downstairs.

The old mansion sat at the very edge of Willow Hollow, surrounded by twisted trees and tangled vines. Most kids stayed away because it looked so spooky.

But tonight, the mansion glowed with beautiful, stolen moonlight.

Ben swallowed nervously. "Maybe this wasn't such a good idea."

Whiskers darted ahead and squeezed through a broken door into the mansion.

"Whiskers, wait!" Ben called. "Come back!"

The door creaked open wider, as if inviting him inside.

Ben took a deep breath. "Here goes nothing."

He stepped inside.

The mansion wasn't as scary as Ben expected. Sure, there were cobwebs and dust everywhere, but the moonlight made everything magical. It sparkled on the walls, floors, and old chandeliers like fairy dust.

And right in the middle of it all floated a small, cheerful ghost!

The ghost was giggling happily, holding the jar full of glowing moonlight. He looked about Ben's age, with sparkly eyes and a warm, friendly smile.

Whiskers sat calmly on the dusty floor, watching the ghost with curiosity instead of fear.

Ben stepped forward bravely. "Hey! That's our moonlight!"

The ghost spun around in the air, startled. "Oh! I didn't steal it! I only borrowed it! My name is Glimmer."

Ben folded his arms. "Well, you need to give it back. The whole town needs it."

Glimmer floated lower, looking sad. "But I needed it too! My house was so dark and lonely. Look how pretty everything is now!"

Ben looked around. The old mansion really did look beautiful in the moonlight. Even the dusty paintings on the walls seemed to smile.

"I understand," Ben said gently. "But without the moonlight, people can't see at night. Owls can't hunt. Fireflies won't come out. And everything is just so dark and sad."

Glimmer's glow dimmed sadly. "I didn't think about that. I was just so tired of being alone in the dark."

Ben felt sorry for the lonely ghost. "What if we found another way to light up your house? Then you could return the moonlight."

Glimmer's eyes sparkled with hope. "Really? You'd help

me?"

Ben smiled. "Of course! Follow me!"

Ben led Glimmer and Whiskers back through town, straight to Mrs. Maple's garden. Rows of bright orange pumpkins sat waiting for Halloween, gleaming in Ben's flashlight beam.

Glimmer's eyes went wide with wonder. "Do these glow too?"

"They will when we carve them!" Ben explained excitedly. "They're called jack-o'-lanterns. If we put some around your house, you'll have light every night without needing to borrow the moonlight."

Glimmer floated in excited circles around the pumpkins. "I love them already!"

"Let's ask Mrs. Maple," Ben said.

Mrs. Maple was delighted to help when they knocked on her door. "I always wondered who lived in that old mansion," she said kindly. "How lovely to meet such a friendly ghost!"

She gave them a whole wagon full of pumpkins and helped them carve happy, glowing faces into each one. She even added candles to make them shine.

Back at the mansion, Glimmer carefully placed jack-o'-lanterns on every windowsill, along the stairs, and beside the front door. Soon, the whole house glowed with warm, cheerful orange light.

"It's perfect!" Glimmer twirled with joy. "Even better

than moonlight because it's mine to keep forever!"

Ben grinned. "And now the town can have its moonlight back."

Glimmer looked at the moonlight jar, then nodded. "You're right. It's time to return what I borrowed."

He floated high above Willow Hollow, carrying the jar carefully. Then he opened it wide.

WHOOSH!

The moonlight rushed back to the sky like a river of silver magic. The full moon returned to its proper place and smiled down at the town below.

The river sparkled again. Rooftops shone brightly. Fireflies danced in the air like tiny, twinkling stars.

Everything was right again.

"That feels much better," Glimmer said, floating back down with a happy sigh.

"Thank you for understanding," Ben said. "And for returning the moonlight."

Glimmer beamed. "Thank YOU for helping me! I'm not lonely anymore, and my house is more beautiful than ever."

Ben smiled warmly. "That's what friends do. But next time you need something, just ask first, okay?"

Glimmer giggled. "I promise! Want to visit my jack-o'-lantern house tomorrow? We could carve even more pumpkins!"

"I'd love to!" Ben said.

Whiskers purred loudly, as if to say, "Mission complete!"

As they walked home under the returned moonlight, Ben felt proud and happy. He'd saved the moonlight, helped a lonely ghost, and made a wonderful new friend.

And Glimmer's mansion, with its warm jack-o'-lantern glow, became the coziest, friendliest house in all of Willow Hollow.

As for the moon? It shone brightly every night and never went missing again.

THE INVISIBLE TRICK-OR-TREATER

Sammy loved Halloween more than any other day of the year. He loved the spooky decorations and glowing jack-o'-lanterns on porches. But the best part was watching kids run from house to house collecting candy.

But Sammy had a big problem.

He was a ghost.

And ghosts couldn't go trick-or-treating.

Every Halloween night, Sammy floated over the neighborhood watching kids dressed as pirates, princesses, and superheroes race from door to door with their treat bags. He watched them laugh, shout "Trick or treat!" and skip away with bags full of delicious candy.

"I wish I could go trick-or-treating too," Sammy sighed, making the leaves swirl around him. "It's not fair that ghosts can't have Halloween fun!"

When Sammy floated to Mrs. Peterson's front porch, he watched a group of costumed kids ring the doorbell.

"Trick or treat!" they all shouted.

"Trick or treat!" Sammy called out too, floating right beside them.

Mrs. Peterson opened the door with a big smile and a bowl full of candy. "Well, hello there, little monsters! You all look wonderful!"

She dropped candy into each kid's bag, but of course, she couldn't see Sammy.

"Hey!" Sammy waved his ghostly arms. "I'm here too!"

But Mrs. Peterson closed the door, and the other kids ran to the next house.

Sammy sank down, feeling as gloomy as a rain cloud. "This is the worst Halloween ever."

Just then, he noticed a girl sitting on the porch next door. She was dressed as a detective, complete with a magnifying glass and a special flashlight. But she wasn't trick-or-treating. Instead, she was shining her flashlight on different things, like the mailbox, a garden gnome, and even a black cat that wandered by.

"That's strange," Sammy thought, floating closer. "What is she doing?"

Suddenly, the girl aimed her flashlight directly at him.

"Oh my goodness!" she gasped. "A real ghost!"

Sammy nearly fell out of the air. "You can see me?!"

The girl nodded excitedly, her eyes wide with wonder. "Yes! I really can! My name is Maya. What's yours?"

"I'm Sammy!" He spun happily in the air. "You're the

first person who's ever seen me! How is this possible?"

Maya held up her flashlight proudly. "This was my grandmother's. She told me it was special and could help me see hidden things. I thought she was kidding, but... wow!"

Sammy's ghostly eyes filled with hope. "Maya, can you please help me? I've wanted to go trick-or-treating my whole life, but nobody can see me!"

Maya thought for a moment, then grinned. "What if we go trick-or-treating together? You could be my partner!"

"But I'm invisible!" Sammy cried. "How would that work?"

Maya's eyes lit up with an idea. "What if... what if my flashlight could make you visible to everyone else too?"

Sammy's ghostly heart leaped with excitement. "Do you think it would work?"

"There's only one way to find out!" Maya turned a small dial on the side of the flashlight.

Suddenly, a warm, golden light wrapped around Sammy like a cozy blanket. He felt tingly all over, and when he looked at his hands, they weren't see-through anymore!

"It worked!" Sammy shouted joyfully. "I'm visible! I'm really, truly visible!"

Maya clapped her hands. "You look just like any other kid! Now let's go get some candy!"

They hurried together to the first house, giggling with

excitement. When the door opened, Sammy took a deep breath.

"Trick or treat!" he called out.

The man at the door smiled. "Well, aren't you two adorable? What are you dressed as?"

Sammy panicked for a second since he didn't have a costume, but then he had a funny idea.

"I'm a ghost!" he said with a grin.

The man chuckled. "Very realistic! Here you go." He dropped candy into both their bags.

Sammy stared at the real candy in his hands. "Maya, I got candy! I actually got candy!"

They went from house to house trick-or-treating, collecting chocolate bars, gummy bears, and lollipops. Sammy had never been so happy in his entire ghostly life.

But as they reached the last house on the street, Maya noticed something.

"Uh oh," she said, looking at her flashlight. "The light is getting dimmer."

Sammy looked down at his hands. They were starting to become see-through again!

"Oh no!" he said. "The magic is wearing off!"

"Quick!" Maya called. "One more house!"

They rushed to the final house, and a kind older woman opened the door.

"Trick or treat!" they both shouted.

The woman smiled warmly. "A detective and a ghost! How wonderful! Take two pieces each."

As Sammy reached for his candy, the golden light flickered and went out. The moment the woman closed the door, he was invisible again.

"Sammy?" Maya called, looking around. "Where did you go?"

"I'm right here," Sammy's voice said softly. "I'm invisible again."

Maya felt sad for her new friend. "I'm sorry the magic didn't last longer."

"It's okay," Sammy said, and Maya could hear the smile in his voice. "That was the best Halloween ever! I got to go trick-or-treating and made my first real friend."

Maya smiled too. "We'll always be friends, Sammy. And you know what? Next year, we can figure out how to make the flashlight work longer."

"Really?" Sammy's voice sounded hopeful.

"Really!" Maya held up her treat bag. "Besides, I think I got way too much candy for just one person. Want to share?"

Sammy laughed happily, the sound floating through the Halloween air. "Thank you, Maya. You made my Halloween dream come true."

As Maya walked home, she wasn't alone. An invisible friend floated beside her, and they were already making plans for next year's Halloween adventure.

Because sometimes, the best friends are the ones you never expected to find.

THE MAGICAL FLOATING HAT

Toby loved autumn days at Maple Park. The golden leaves crunched under his sneakers as he threw a stick for Rascal, his tiny terrier.

"Go get it, boy!" Toby called.

Rascal dashed after the stick, then suddenly stopped. His ears perked up, and he tilted his head toward the playground.

"What is it, Rascal?" Toby asked.

Rascal pointed his nose at something floating near the swing sets. A large, black top hat was spinning through the air all by itself!

Toby's eyes went wide. "Is that hat... flying?"

Rascal barked excitedly. Woof! Woof!

The hat swooped in circles, then zigzagged toward the picnic tables. Toby and Rascal followed, amazed.

"Wait up, magical hat!" Toby called.

The hat drifted down beneath a huge oak tree and landed with a soft plop.

"Maybe it's tired?" Toby whispered.

A small voice groaned, "Ugh! This isn't working!"

Toby jumped back. Rascal hid behind his legs.

A tiny, shimmering ghost popped out from under the hat! He had a friendly face and sparkling eyes, but something looked very wrong.

"A real ghost!" Toby gasped.

"Boo," the ghost said weakly. "Sorry, I'm not very good at being scary."

Toby looked closer. "Wait... where's the rest of you?"

The ghost sighed sadly. "That's my problem. I'm just a floating head! My name is Pip."

"Hi, Pip," Toby said kindly. "I'm Toby, and this is Rascal. What happened to your body?"

Pip floated down to the picnic table. "It's almost Halloween, and all my ghost friends were playing hide-and-seek in the old graveyard. I found the perfect hiding spot inside an ancient treasure chest."

"That sounds like a great hiding place," Toby said.

"It was! But when I tried to get out..." Pip looked miserable. "Only my head could fit through the keyhole. The rest of me is still stuck inside!"

Toby's mouth dropped open. "Your body is trapped in a treasure chest?"

"Yes! Tomorrow night is the Big Halloween Parade. All the ghosts in town march together, and I've been looking forward to it all year!" Ghostly tears sparkled in Pip's eyes. "But who wants to see just a floating head in a hat?"

Rascal whimpered sympathetically.

Toby thought hard. "Maybe we can help you get your body back!"

Pip's face brightened. "Really? You'd do that for me?"

"Of course! Friends help friends," Toby said. "But first, where is this treasure chest?"

Pip's expression fell. "That's the problem. The graveyard is huge, and I can't remember where I hid. Plus, it's hard to search without hands!"

Toby looked around the park, thinking carefully. Then his face lit up. "What if we can't find your real body in time? Maybe we could make a temporary one for you!"

"What do you mean?" Pip asked curiously.

Toby pointed to an old scarecrow near the community garden. "We could fix up that scarecrow! Then you'd have a body for the parade!"

Pip gasped. "That's brilliant! But will it work?"

"Let's find out!" Toby said excitedly.

They hurried over to the forgotten scarecrow. It looked pretty shabby, with torn clothes and straw poking out everywhere.

"He needs some work," Toby admitted. "But I have an idea!"

Toby ran to the park's lost-and-found box. Inside, he found a cozy blue jacket, warm gloves, and some gently worn boots.

"These are perfect!" he exclaimed.

Toby carefully dressed the scarecrow while Rascal helped by holding things in his mouth. They put on the jacket, gloves, and boots, tying everything securely. Pip's hat sat perfectly on top.

"Now for the most important part," Toby said. "Pip, try floating down onto the shoulders!"

Pip took a deep breath, even though ghosts don't really breathe. "Here goes nothing!"

He gently settled onto the scarecrow's shoulders. Suddenly, a warm, tingly feeling spread through the straw body.

Pip blinked. Then he wiggled his fingers. Then he stomped his feet.

"It works!" Pip shouted, jumping up and down. "I can feel everything! I have hands! I have feet!"

Toby and Rascal cheered. "Hooray!"

Pip spun around, his new jacket fluttering in the breeze. "This is amazing! I feel like a real ghost again!"

The next evening, Main Street was packed with people for the Halloween Parade. Witches cackled, vampires swirled their capes, and mummies shuffled along. Music filled the air, and everyone was having a wonderful time.

Pip marched proudly with the ghost group, wearing his scarecrow body. He waved to all the children lining the sidewalk. "Happy Halloween!" he called cheerfully.

Toby and Rascal watched from the crowd, beaming with pride.

When Pip spotted them, he tipped his hat gratefully. "Thank you!" he called. "This is the BEST HALLOWEEN EVER!"

After the parade ended, Pip found Toby at the park.

"I have good news!" Pip said happily. "Some of my ghost friends heard about my problem. They're going to help me find the treasure chest tomorrow!"

"That's wonderful!" Toby said. "But what about your scarecrow body?"

Pip smiled warmly. "Well, I'd like to keep it as a backup. You know, for special occasions?"

Toby grinned. "I think that's a great idea. Friends should always be prepared!"

Rascal barked in agreement.

As the moon rose over Maple Park, Pip carefully placed his scarecrow body back in the community garden where they'd found it. But now it looked neat and cared for, ready and waiting for the next adventure.

OTHER BOOKS BY AUTHOR

(AVAILABLE & COMING SOON)

1) Yes! You Are an Amazing Girl (6-12)

2) Yes! You Are an Amazing Black Girl (6-12)

3) Yes! You Are an Amazing Black Boy (6-12)

4) Yes! You Are an Amazing Boy (6-12)

5) Yes! Brave, Bold, Blonde, That's Me (6-12)

6) Yes! We Are Amazing Girls Around the World

7) Pony Tales: Stories for Young Riders (7-12)

8) Fun Bedtime Stories for Younger Kids (4-6)

9) Fun Bedtime Stories for Older Kids (7-10)

10) Campfire Stories for Kids (8-12)

11) Lights Off: Spooky Stories for Kids(8-12)

12) Whooo! Grins and Goosebump

Vol. 1: Spooky Stories for Kids (5-8)

13) Whooo! Giggles and Shivers

Vol. 2: More Spooky Stories for Kids (5-8)

14) Short Stories for Seniors

15) A Little Elf Tobin: A Fantasy Adventure

www.ingramcontent.com/pod-product-compliance
Lightning Source LLC
Chambersburg PA
CBHW062147160726
48282CB00027B/956
9789355252814